Ariana Olisvos
Her Last Works
and Days

David Dwyer

UNIVERSITY OF MASSACHUSETTS PRESS 1976

Acknowledgments

Special thanks, for a grant-in-aid, to the Mary Roberts Rinehart Foundation.

For permission to reprint the following poems: "Prologue" and "Dreamt Afterwords," copyright © 1973, 1974 by the *New York Quarterly;* "In the Enemy Camp" and "A Witch-Song," copyright © 1976 by the *South Dakota Review;* "On Her Birthday," copyright © 1974 by the *Iowa Review;* "Near Death" (originally entitled "Poem Near Death") and "Persephone," copyright © 1974 by *Aphra,* the Feminist Literary Magazine. Concerning the last two poems:

In 1973 and 1974 David Dwyer wrote a series of letters to *Aphra* presenting himself as a 92-year-old woman poet. On the strength of this impersonation two of the "Ariana Olisvos" poems were printed in our issue on aging, *Growing Older,* along with excerpts from her supposed letters and the the false biography given therein. The hoax was revealed by a third party and *Aphra* printed an apology to its readers in the following issue.

Because for millenia women artists in the Western world have been denied space in which to express themselves, *Aphra* was dedicated to the theory and practice of feminist art in 1969. With the whole world open to him, we find David Dwyer's fradulent entry into our enclave morally and politically offensive and artistically distasteful. —The Editors of *Aphra*

All that is personal soon rots . . . it
must be packed in ice or salt.
—Yeats

Contents

V

VI

Ariana Olisvos

Her Last Works
and Days

Prologue

Numbers are no one's age. It is true
I was born on July 22nd in eighteen
hundred and eighty-one, but that
is nowhere near how old I am.
                            Numbers are not
how old anyone is. Since that day,
I have married and traveled and married again
and had children and friends and grandchildren,
even a lover or so . . .
                    la la
                            . . . and once,
at Covent Garden, Mr. Swinburne
bowed to me, or to my sister, and
we both curtsied back and that
is exactly how old I am.
                            Before
this century began, I made
some faërie stories Mr. Lang
thought well of and the men
who printed them and sold them and the children
who drifted asleep with those books in their arms
are all, nearly all, worm farms now,
or stripped too bare to be maggots' meat.

And all those absences and bones
are how old I am.
                    I have tried to survive
and keep track of my life, I have tried to deal
with each year as it came over me,
and have failed . . . and all those names
and faces have become my age.
                            And everyone
I used to know has gone into the darkness
and my hands quiver with the grief of their
departures, my lovers and my friends no more.
For a very long time now, from when
I was a little child, I have been
dying, and that is exactly how old I am.

I

The world was very old, indeed,
when you and I were young . . .
—G.K. Chesterton

If, in a time, you will be done with me,
    whatever you and I have done
and will have then forgotten, do not say
    any kindhearted, subtle thing.

I will not understand. I will be dense
    as our lilacs were this fiery May
just over, when their blue weight filled our house.
    And, whatever's done, I will not be.

Before a Storm

Maintenant? maintenant? the french window
creaks and, across the lawn,
(where your bare feet have barely now
stopped muttering *Away,*
turn away in the charged grass) the chair
you were sitting in begins
to whimper and explain. The warped screen door
stutters and snarls *G-g-go!*

The house and all the things about
the house speak in the voice of your going.
Our disenchanted cat
stares after you and then she stares at me
and *Hush!* she says *Enough, enough of that.*

A Postcard I Once Meant to Write

You ask, did I love you?
(Already, they tell me, you've lost that quick
conspiratorial grin my name,
overheard, used to sketch on your otherwise quite
unmemorable face.)

You ask, did I love you? (Damn,
but the flesh is a goddamn shame.)
Ah, damn, I shall go someplace . . .

Relax: I shall go to a secret place,
now I've forgotten whose secret I am,
and burn your letters.

I loved you. I loved you. Forget it.

Persephone

My little sister was the pretty one; the Pumpkin,
she was called—as if we knew
her name was magical and not for use.

The Pumpkin was the pretty one (though I
was thought "not plain") and I have down
in an old diary, and just now shivered with the old
bitter rage to read, that Mother whispered
once to me: "I wonder . . ."

(She had come on me picking my way
through a chorus of Aeschylus
by the garden window, her arms
full of yellow flowers.)

              ". . . I wonder,
Ariana, if there's Greek enough
for you to learn in the whole world,"
she whispered, handing me a flower
as if by mistake,
              ". . . Greek enough
to match the fall of that black
hair down over your sister's
shivery white breast . . ."

There was not, as it happens.

We had lessons and secrets together,
till the Pumpkin turned seventeen and took
the full burden of her loveliness dutifully
into a dull marriage. I learned more Greek.
I learned a great many things.

She has been gone and ugly now so long,
firestormed in the second war, and rotting
underfoot so many years that sometimes
I can almost wish her dead.

8

Sonnet After an Image of Mrs. Browning's

Neither your hands nor mine cast any light
nor the unstarred night at the window,
not our mouths even, so if we thought
we might finally see each other,
we may have been wrong.
      (Though we empty
our hearts to fill the blind
flesh, kiss open its eyes, though we try
to learn by touch a spell
to keep off morning and the world, Thérèse,
Thérèse, they both will dawn again.)

Or say that we overlooked each other? say (darkness
by darkness) we have only found
a momentary private place? never had our day?
Or say that we loved each other, but we lost our way.

They always want to stand, like words,
between us and the world.

"You are the first," I said to him
(only to please, though it was true).
"You are the first man,
perhaps the only I shall ever know."
(And that, too, only to please,
though—oddly—I must have believed it.)

And other things I said to other men
to please them, though—oddly—
not only that . . .
                    So often,
a thing I said, perhaps, to move
some heavyhanded heart
out from between the world
and me—or, perhaps, to please him,
though not only that . . . the words
so often turned out true.

How quick the sadness was to grow;
how quickly, like a string
of traps, the years have sprung.
But the getting out of words,
that was so slow.

Perch'i' non spero di tornar giammai . . .

In the end she will be found
more beautiful than not, all lovers
that were lovers lost and having lost
all friends, all influence, she will be thought
rather a lady in the aftermath,
for certain graces in her hands, for how
the edgy feeling of her voice
would sometimes fail, for all her mastering it;
how, treated gently, she was sometimes kind,
betrayed and turned upon, a woman still
of the purest clarity of mind.

Often I've whispered her name and
others perhaps even more often said
how the eyes and faintly crooked fingers
were passionate, impassioned, never warm;
and the small mouth . . .
                   It is a woman's face
out of my childhood and the horned past,
a dear face dearly found more beautiful than not . . .

11

Eden, 1899: Sonnet plus cruel que symboliste

On ne peut vraiment voir la ville du
coeur qu'en la revisitant comme orphelin
et veuf—ou bien, comme Ange . . .

Je ne regrette ni la sève
Dont tu fus le vampire, ni
Les os-de-coeur auxquels, comme Eve
A l'hameçon divin,
Délicatement tu mordis,
Toi, l'Autre et la Lointaine.

D'abord, je t'aimai; tu m'aimas.
Mais l'hameçon fut une pomme
de discorde et tu ne fus pas
seulement l'Autre et la Lointaine,
Tu fus aussi
Mon Ange qui
Devenit homme.

Moi, je regrette le jardin.

Eden, 1899: A Sonnet More Cruel Than Symbolist

One cannot truly see the city of the heart,
except by revisiting it orphaned and widowed
—or as an Angel . . .

I do not miss the sap of which you were the vampire, nor the heart's-bones
at which, as Eve did at the divine bait, you delicately nibbled, you, the
Other and the Far-away. At first, I loved you; you loved me. But the bait
was an apple of discord and you were not only the Other and the Far-away,
you were also my Angel who turned human. As for me, what I miss is
the garden.

12

Dreamt Afterwords

I have been loved by something strange . . .
and it has forgotten me.
—Djuna Barnes

. . . the sweet first schoolgirl love affair
went on, and Caitlin never sent to me
those anonymous red murdered roses,
I never wrote her that cruel Symbolist sonnet,
never called her a vampire. Turning eighteen,
we did not turn from one another, but I still kept
a place at my ridiculous small breasts
for her mouth, and years and years we went on opening
our hearts and thighs to one another only.

I never switched allegiance, never went
flightily into the desert with my Foreign Legionnaire.
And the newspapers lied a few weeks later,
sketching her in eighteen yards of Alençon,
in the arms of an up-and-coming New York lawyer.
They lied, to the last detail of lace and pink
champagne. They lied. And the Army accounts for eighteen
ninety-nine that show Augustus Keller
made a major and married to an Irish-American
virgin are partly false;
                    I was not there.

Caitlin and I had gone away together,
turning eighteen, and worked as *au pair* girls
a year or so at Kingstown Harbour on St. Vincent,
till we bought the inn at Bequia.

We flourished there a half a century,
till, shaking my shoulders fiercely, she died,
her nails sunk in me as she shivered out . . .

We loved each other all that time.
The rest is lies. Between her white small
body and my leathery legs, arms, breasts,
the snake has never crawled.
                              In our cool open bedroom,
near the sea, the moths and butterflies
beat on the netting over us for fifty years
and we were happy and the rest is lies.

II

The loves we share with a city
are often secret loves.

—Camus

A Letter to My Daughter

There was a way we lived (not at all as I have
these last years, though just a quick
catch of the breath better . . .), before you were born,
but I do not anymore want to tell it over . . .

At Sidi-bel-Abbès, it was mostly dust; and, later,
on Guadeloupe, spiders like gods . . .

                                It is true,
I have memories of islands and desert towns
as sharp as your memories of me . . .

                                And now, behind Honolulu,
the houses partly climb the long fingers
of one distracted mountain and, standing on Waikiki
to watch the sun go into Barbers Point,
I remember a phrase of Lucretius'—*ad luminis oras*—
and remember: Now I live, alone and as I will,
in one of those high fields of light . . .
                        And,
you see, I do not anymore want
to tell it all over, not even to you: how I sip
dry sherry evenings now and care
nothing for expense—where, at Sidi-bel-Abbès,
I was permitted beer but had to scrimp
for it; how it was not all dust . . .

                          Your father
was much away; he imagined himself "a leader
of men"—which is exactly what he was.
I sat on our porch and sipped beer, reading Homer.
And all their wars went on . . .
                     Still, dawn,
when it came, broke open like a rose,
and it came too soon.

Sidi-bel-Abbès

The young ones always ask me: What was
Casablanca like? I never
went there; my whole mind
turned on the fighting and the weather
to the south, around Fort Mac-Mahon.

Jack Olisvos courted me all the hot winter
of nineteen hundred/nineteen one,
while the desert absorbed my husband
until he blurred with the sand somewhere
between the Fort and Timimoun.
Then Jack and I had all our time
before us and no time for romantic
sidetrips, both of us wanting the sea.

Even my daughter, the major's daughter,
asked me once: "It was only a few hundred miles. . . ?"
"Six hundred and seventy-six kilometers,"
I told her, "overland; I never went there."

1900

I thought I could betray a friend and lie
   quiet in desert starlight
with the Lord of Stars (as he seemed to me).
   I could not sleep that night.

I could not sleep for many nights;
   the stars all hissed at me:
It is right if you think it's right—
   we never said it was easy.

For Major Keller

Every day we go farther, but never advance.
Simple things: you when you flowered first
in my mind, then in me. (I was very young;
we were very young.)
                    So we made
love and made a child, my love, and got
nowhere.
                When I said I would die for you,
I did not know how very long it would take.

            You see—dear faceless
unforgotten young love and lover,
sixty-some sweet years rotten—
I've studied all this while pursuing you
and only just begun to get it right.

Other Cities

I

In Cambridge, at The Plough and Stars, in 1923,
I was taught, one afternoon, the meaning
of things, what keeps the stars from devouring
one another, and the moon from falling on us;
why cats, and some people, wash before killing;
(I took notes on a menu); how love convinces
some to stay and some to leave; why flowers
work, despite their inefficient architecture;
this and a great deal more.
      I treasured that menu.
It was more to me than love letters, baby pictures,
checkbooks and diplomas. Then the war came
and a firebomb took it from me, exactly
as it had predicted.
      Desolation and fire
were part of the explanation I'd been given.

II

I went back then with you, that late
summer, where you had never been,
where I had never been with you.
I was so serious when I first found
that city, ages before the Dutch disease
had stripped its whispering streets . . .
      Betrayed,
they would say, *betrayed and our secrets told . . .*

We bowed to each other; our fingers met
high in air like moths dancing
and fell away; we walked in step
down Westcott Street in the green and unforgiving
light, beneath the memory of elms.

III

... or, as if we two could saddle up
great black dreamhorses and ride out
alone to the beautiful place, its ruins,
just after the fall of an ancient empire.

And whispering and whispering to each other, we came
through broken marble steps and things
to the last garden and lay down.
We lay down helpless in the dusty grass;
my fingers slipped on the sweat on your shoulders,
then caught, your hair in my eyes ...

                                             The farmers
had all gone off to war in the south.
In the trelliswork above us,
the black grapes began to swell and burst.

Archaeology

Nothing has ever "vanished without a trace."

Dreamt-of, unremembered cities secrete
artifacts to take the measure of our
thinskinned imperishable loneliness,
growing in earth smoothedged as old affairs.

And we dig in each other's hearts for hidingplace.

A Sonnet in Sprung Alexandrines

Whether forevered or whiled away, my mother's times
are over and the white stars click into place, night
opens abruptly as a cat yawns.

                             Against the morphine's
ringing, tumult of Demerol and her own bones, she brought
to bear foreknowledge of some voracious mercy and she drew
the waste of flesh and mind together, caving around
the mushroom tumor, until her shoulders rounded, humped,
her hands clawed over; she became, for a time, "birdlike,"
    as swàns do.

We are touched
              and wonder who could reach us, wonder how she,
who was almost close enough to touch, became instead
an irrecoverably far thing.
                    My mother, though a few parishes pray
for *Rita-our-sister-who-sleeps,* is not fallen in dreams. She is dead.
And she knew that, as she knew the heavens. She had discovered
    night and learned,
when at last she found the starlight blinding, that it would not
    burn.

Elegy: Lines Left Out of the Foregoing Sonnet

Probably, my mother thought
all pity of the dying
pitiable. She had worked out
a place in her mind for the pain
that otherwise had forced her
to bury all sense in morphine;
she'd decided (near death) that she'd weather
death's every stratagem,
unbroken and uncorrupted. "Really,"
she'd whisper, "I'm a braver woman
than I sound . . ." So we felt almost silly,
giving her tears, when
(hollow of bone as any bird,
cut, wrinkled, and eaten-
inside by her cancer) she found it hard
as ever to smile and take them.

So she humored us and humored the-worm-
in-her-flesh-before-it-died,
and we felt almost we had done her harm
by weeping. If she ever cried,
it was not for the fact, but for the mystery:
how we go unexplained from here
to silence. My mother was never a grave woman,
and I would pray for her no resurrection,
but that she comprehend
(as she would wish to) every change
and process of her dissolution;
that the pine and concrete rot,
the fluids dry, and let
her flesh be no more lonely for the world;
that if (after our long rage and longer silence)
the universe can still contrive to sing,
its music echo to the end of things
still in the ravaged caverns of her heart.

III

Aimai-je un rêve?

—Mallarmé

The Lioness and the Unicorn
(from *An Amorous History of the Beasts*)

First the cat-stretching, kittenish
play of the golden muscles;
she is self-absorbed and feels
only a lioness in the flesh . . .

At first, the unicorn would only peek
his head around the roses,
study her long insouciant thighs,
the great chest and cat's-poses . . .

"Ideas of what's fantastic," the lioness
remarked to the quivering underbrush,
"and though fantastic beautiful, most often
polarize
between red roses and your own
imaginary species . . ."

He trotted out to her.
"*Imagined* is a better word, my dear."
"Perhaps."
⠀⠀⠀⠀⠀She purred it at him and he silverpawed
the morningsilvered grass in answer.
⠀⠀⠀⠀⠀⠀⠀⠀⠀⠀"Ondines, nereids,
and water-nymphs pertain to the *imaginary*
genera, the dear
unmanageables, alas . . ."

⠀⠀⠀⠀⠀⠀⠀⠀⠀"You rhapsodize," she grumbled.

"... and the unattained. Well,
each of us has loved a mermaid—till he won her
and discovered
he could no more desire her
than desire a fish. Still, her going under
(and I speak with special reference), her
going off affected me, as the deaths in
far-off places of those once-friends-not-known-
some-years. She was a pleasurable woman,
more easily dismayed than angered . . ."

"So are all women, handled properly . . ."

"I was not proper . . . I was eloquent."

"... *and you'd've had her, but her heart was spent.*
I know the old songs, unicorn . . ."

The unicorn wrinkled his nose and whinnied, "I
would remind you, Lady, that a man may live
in time of need or time of war
on cat's-meat and you hold
your dispensation from the feast
on purely economic grounds . . ."

                    "I am big but beautiful,"
she growled into his ear, "much more to look at
than devour."

                    "Myself," he said, not hearing her,
"well, for myself, I relate
more to the work of Fabergé than to plain nature.
I am the ultimate knick-knack . . ."

                    "Beauty," the lioness huffed,
"owes *something* to its followers . . ."

                    "No, no, my dear,
I am not *beautiful.* Big cats
are *beautiful . . .* and subject to be eaten for it."

"A clever phrase,"
she smirked, "but *qui vivra*—you'll pardon
my ferocious *r*'s—*verra*."

                    "Observe," he said
and reared up over her, "the gimcrack horn
and sterling silver hooves. I am grown
fabulously inedible, no use at all to kill."

                    The lioness
stretched with conscious elegance beneath him
and whistled a bit of *L'Après-Midi.*

                    "Lady,"
he snorted, straddling her, "it is a well-known fact
that cats can't whistle."

                    "It's as well
or better known—grasseater!
nibble-a-daisy!—that only carnivores
can talk . . . or think, at least, of anything to say."

"Puss, you are not fair . . . and, oh, how ponderous
in your cat's-eyes are questions
simple as a mouse," he said as he knelt
on his trembling forelegs beside her.

                         She tickled his nose
with the tip of her tail. "Well, pretty unic',"
she half-purred into the white haunch she had begun
to lick with kisses, "just as censors must
in conscience be censorious, and merchants
mercantile, I'm some such adjective
of hunger . . ."

          He sighed and ran his tongue
and cold black nose along her spine. "Now, which
of your graces, I wonder, are feline
and which deliberate?"

31

"*Grrrrrrrrrrrf!* will you spend
all your life finding out where you live?
Come into me, horse,"
she nuzzled him and murmured in his ear.

Toward dusk, while the lioness lolled in his garden
and played at boxing with a butterfly
as grey as the light, the shaken unicorn
patrolled his country's borders ill-at-ease.

          "Lie quiet, unicorn,"
she grumbled after him. He froze, turned back
to her.

          "Lady, you know, tomorrow morning
I shall be twenty-six hundred
and eight years old . . ."

          "Silly immortalist,
lie down! Can you not pretend—
as I do pretend—that you live with your
monstrous lover in a crewel dream
and have no substance but silk floss
and wool on linen?"

          "Well, comfort me
with French-knot kisses, Lady," he said
as he tucked himself into her shadow,
"for my laid-stitch heart is sore . . ."

"Ahhhhhh,
Sing a song o'baby's-breath,"
she mumbled and closed her eyes,
"*a penny for your thoughts . . .*
after the first o'many deaths,
it hardly ever hurts . . ."

The beast hid when I was a child
in the pattern of a rug or hunched
against a half-familiar skyline.
Now it lies down with me in one
two-backed beast; now we spit
and claw each other, now lick our wounds,
each other's wounds, lie down again,
and snarl and purr and scratch and sleep.

The Old Symbolist's Song
Against This Present Age

The 20th century's done me ill,
I sometimes think, though what
I'd hoped it'd do me I can't recall.
The times and I forget
each other a little more every day
and yet a little while
ye see me and yet again
a little while ye may
see less of me, and just as well.

Oh, I wish I were drinking champagne,
in bed with Gérard de Nerval.

IV

To (Be) or Not to (Be)

To (Be) or Not to (Be)
(excerpts from Cantos i-vi)
from the Turkish of Murad Osman-Talaat

Canto One

The alterego(is)ts live in glass houses & dre(am) they see
themselves as others see them, never guess
their gross perspective, circled as they (are) in semimirrors,
has merits all its own.
                              First, (be)fore everything,
they seek to contribute to the eventual degradation—
which their holy books have clearly prophesied—of
the verb *to (be). Das (Sein). L' (être).* They desire
nothing less than the absolute d(is)appearance of that un-
mentionable in whose complete denial Immanuel Kant
has said there (is) no contradiction.
                              But having striven
blind centuries—father to son—at th(is), they
realize stopgap measures must often suffice . . .

Canto Two

To (be) an alterego(is)t (is), after all, not wholly
to submerge one's self in
otherness; it (is) more a bapt(is)m. And now
these fellows see the labors of a dozen gener-
ations bandied about in (Am)erican universities—even
at Ro(be)rt College here in (Is)tanbul they toy
with reality & with fresh usages—& the alterego(is)ts
(are) ill-at-ease.
                    They *hope* they have planted
the seed of a new semantics in the new world.
They do not hope too much, though, having found
their own experiments with one another
arduous in the extreme . . .

37

They have endeavoured each
to come into another's nature, as Dickens' characters
come sometimes into long-contested legacies,
modestly & with (be)coming grace; they have found th(is)
more difficult than it sounds. They have found
it—so far—impossible . . .

Canto Three

Wherever you go you meet alterego(is)ts.
                                        It would
astound you to learn how close to the truth that
hyperbole comes. They have, you see, no d(is)tingu(is)hing
marks, unless one gets to know them intimately.
They wear the clothing & the smiles of the middle
of the middle-class of whatever place they hap-
pen "momentarily" to inhabit.
                            Alterego(is)ts speak
of their lives & those of their pre-
decessors as "moments"—th(is) (is) almost their
sole affectation, th(is) & the matter of the verb *to (be)*.
Still, they leave traces. . . .

                        One never, for ex(am)ple, sees
an alterego(is)t in church, unless for an organ recital.
Religion appears to them mainly an outdoor activity. None-
theless, the alterego(is)ts love g*d with an aim—
less fervor they realize can lead them
only to despair or to salvation.
                        They (are) not
concerned with details, but with ends . . . "the ends
of (being)" really, though they would not
phrase it thus. . . .
                    Life, as they imagine others
lead it, often momentarily entices them, but they
take comfort in other
imaginings, futurity. . . .

Canto Four

Their methods of constructing controversies (are),
like their methods of housebuilding, a source
of confusion to aliens.
                    They say, for ex(am)ple, that
a subway station (is) a legitimate analogy for living,
since one grows lonely sometimes waiting no more
than a minute for trains one has certainty of catching.
It seems to them hopeless to stand in a place
designed for departure's natural agonies
and pretend d(is)interest. A method of transposing
flesh, they say, in a flash from one quarter to another
which does not allow for the purchase of round-trip tickets
(is) a metaphysical horror.
                    We do not, they go on,
deserve to get off so easily . . .

Th(is) confusion pleases them
when they reflect on it. They conclude
that their "apprenticeship"—a term for the sum
of past "moments"—has not (been) in vain.
                                    For—
strangest of all, perhaps—nothing fills
an alterego(is)t with more d(is)may than the prospect
that someone may (be) converted
to h(is) way of seeing . . . .

Canto Five

It (is) sometimes maintained by those who do not
know them well that the alterego(is)ts (are) totally
devoid of humor. Nothing could (be) farther
from the truth—& nothing, I need hardly add, (is)
de(are)r to an alterego(is)t's heart than the truth . . .

You often, for ex(am)ple, hear
an older alterego(is)t refer with mock solemnity
to h(is) efforts in (be)half of
the last sultan—by th(is) they intend a theologic
wittic(is)m, since the d(is)establ(is)hment of (Is)l(am)
by the republicans in '28 pleased them immensely. Non-
sense to say they had not foreseen it—they had.
Also—& I heard th(is) from the alterego(is)t chiefly
responsible, now very old but still coherent—they
engineered Ataturk's campaign to
put the Latin alpha(be)t in general use; they felt
& still feel that its angularity & air
of d(is)cretion, as opposed to the sinuous
carnality of the old script, (be)tter
serves the cause of non-(being) . . .

    Canto Six

What the real alterego(is)t wants, though, (is) in-
finitely complex, far (be)yond gr(am)matical
quibbles. They have a drearily complete
progr(am) &, frankly, I who know
more of their schemes than most aliens
(am) every day more (am)azed at the extent to which
their designs have already (been) implemented. Th(is)
also (am)uses them. . . .
                    . . . in fact, though their fingers stick
in innumerable honey-pots, they say they will never
find the world sweet
till it (is) sacr(am)entalized . . . although
they pointedly do not say what they mean by th(is).
They smile & direct one to inscrutable or
unobtainable works of reference; the alterego(is)ts, as
one of them has said to me, (are) the un-
acknowledged librarians of this world.

A note on the translation:

Murad Osman-Talaat (b. 1940), although not yet widely known in the English speaking world, is something of a public institution in his own country, where he writes for several large newspapers under his own name and two or three transparent pseudonyms.

Talaat was educated to join his family's very successful law firm, but he was also permitted easy access to Western literature and ideas from an early age and has a good reading knowledge of several European languages, including English. After practicing law briefly in the mid-sixties, he began to devote his full energies to journalism. He has travelled extensively and spent most of 1967 in America.

The excerpts here given represent about half of the text of the first six cantos of "To (Be) or Not to (Be)" as published in various Turkish newspapers and magazines and are used with the author's permission and approval. The translation retains as much as seems to me possible of the peculiar tone and manner of my peculiar friend's poem. Thus, for example, I have parenthesized *all* forms of the verb *to (be)*, as Talaat does, though these obviously do not fall in the same words in both languages. This and several other dilemmas I am conscious of having more sidestepped than solved.

V

We are not wise
this side of rigor mortis.
—Djuna Barnes

In the Enemy Camp

"Practice makes perfect," the nuns in grammar school said.
And then I came to know a man with a terrible expertise;
given the proper tools, he could kill another
man who, nearly a mile away, was sleeping
or shooting back or breaking the bread that maybe
you or I had handed him.
                              "Do not stay,"
they said, "where you are not wanted." And "*Every* prayer
ought to be one of acceptance."

                              Though we envy the sniper
his skill, even he cannot see in the dark. Feed
what bread you have to the shape across the fire
and slip away to a place you can almost believe
is yours; bury within whatever light
you've brought away; wait there.

Dream: Over the River
(from *An Amorous History of the Beasts*)

In the name of the Father I cross myself
and of the Son they cannot cross
and of the Holy Spirit running
water can they no I now
take up this is the body and wine
of the new and eternal they cannot bear
even wild garlic wild raw
roses I now shed this silver
cross they cannot cross they are not
like the dead we walk on in the name
of silver I now take and drink
of this is my blood of the new and for you
and for bloody many take it and cross
myself cross water . . .

And down the long bridge he comes to me.

A Witch-Song

For Mirabelle de l'Anclos of the first
sisterhood who taught me in childhood
to play the cat-piano and to cast the
simpler runes, who- and wherever she
now may be: *Denn die Todten reiten
schnell— For the dead travel fast* . . .

First the knife goes in, and then
the heart goes out;
next the salt, and once again
the light goes out.

Ask Mirabelle: How goes the trade?
How goes her dancing tongue?
Who can unmake what the knife has made?
Who but a fool would stay young?

Ask Mirabelle, and she replies:
*As quick the bloody heart,
so quick the knife, so quick the trade
to finish what its daughters start.*

*Sweet though the morning is,
the night was sweeter;
fast though the horses of desire,
the knife and the wolves are faster.*

Ask Mirabelle (who had a choice)
why time has slowed her tongue . . .
Why did she turn the casting-voice
on every enemy but age?

The night, says Mirabelle,
*is sweeter—and how else assuage
the bloody heart? how else
but let it wither?*

47

Fast though the unicorn springs
over the snows of this world's winter,
faster the wolves will follow
and the knife will have his tongue . . .

Sweet though the morning was,
who but a fool would stay young?

Holy Ireland

This is my letter to that old country
that's all too often written me
and called long-distance in its cups,
towards dawn . . .

                  Yeats and his friend John Synge
found Ireland's voices helped them find their voice,
but I (though not in everything
of his persuasion, though not
for his gigantic reasons) side here with Mr. Joyce.

I, too, have dreamt and come to light appalled.
I, too, have seen
the strong male nurse he saw in dreams
who helped him follow,
                        long summer afternoons,
the straight path along the garden wall,
behind St. Patrick's
                (behind all
                his dearest assumptions?
                in honored old age,
                if little understood?)
in the great Dean's mad and doddering footsteps.

"James Connolly"
or: The Power of Music

After the Rising and the trial,
it came to him that no revenge
could match that self-satisfied smile
he'd learnt to meet the firing-squad.

Next morning, he stumbled at grave's-edge
back from the bullets and fell into his country,
choking on blood and a lilting phrase
of the coldblooded song he had begun to be.

Memento Mori

The cat's-eye light flits
in and out my blinded
semi-private window. It's
a reminder. I'm reminded.

A Footnote on the Beast Within

The 19th century, said Wilde, was Caliban's rage
before a mirror wherein he sometimes saw
himself and sometimes didn't.
                              Now he prowls his cage
(which sometimes is the world and sometimes isn't),
perplexed at this grim enlightened age
wherein he's sound and the looking-glass is crazed.

De Natura Deorum

(from *An Amorous History of the Beasts*)

Their comings and goings are secret. They send
(when they've something to say) messengers
(Greek: *angels*) who speak (see Swedenborg) the tongues
of men by courtesy. Little is known of their
habits and cities. Many have visited with them
and come home speechless, from which we deduce
what we like. Less numerous now
than formerly, they frequent wildernesses,
forsaking the amenities
for a little peace and quiet. Above all,
as Sappho says, by their disquieting
choice of immortality,
they are the proof that death is evil.

Envoi

It blurs. It drifts. It tastes
of blood. It never
counts the cost.
It blurs. It drifts. It's lost
its only lover.
It keeps its promises. It tastes
of blood. It's young.
It's old.
It's over.

VI

None of us suffers as much as we should,
or loves as much as we say.
—Djuna Barnes

On Her Birthday

The pain never stops.

They dress the nurses in a white
like the wings of yachts or angels
to glitter on the insane-blue
sky-and-water-colored walls.
The crabby old woman
turns a crabbed ninety-two.
("She is resting comfortably,"
says a nurse in the hall.)
But she finds rest
nowhere for her distracted eye.

Though I was born on the cusp of the Lion,
I've been Cancerian from birth
and never Leonine . . .
                              My lust
to have all this all over
drove me (it seems) to grey, straight
out of my black-and-white childhood.

Can she ever have shimmered blonde
a moment in anyone's sight, this old
bitch, old ramblemouth cross-
quaint wrack of a lady?

The nurses, like sails, feed on distance
and glitter more and more as they slip
down the corridor, away, around
the headland out of Port Elizabeth,
into the channel of sunlight . . .

I make no more voyages. I lie up
close with the Crab, and lovingly
he nibbles me—now bone and joint,
now teat, now womb, now brain . . .
(He'll nibble out my heart.)
                                 The pain
never stops. If they tell you it will,
whatever they mean,
they are not your friends.

Sonnet: That Grief
Was Not the Center of My Life

δαύοις ἀπάλας ἑτάρας ἐν στήθεσιν

Under the wind, at Heart's-Rise, morning
webbed first in the spidery pine-branches
over us, climbed down the needles gingerly
point-to-point an hour, and found our bodies
praising each other with sleep, and caught us up.

We had ridden dark out in a curl of the cresting rise,
not even a mountain; we woke as the light was turning
from fiber to foam in the whipped tree-tops,
and made love as strong and feverish as dawn and twittery
as the birds watching us—waxwings and three kinds of finches . . .

I knew all their names then; we knew all the magical names
of real things, and used them. That secret tongue—
with whom should I speak it now? I say over the same
words, in a different language. But I have not forgotten.

Near Death

I

I really think I have never forgotten
anything done me out of passion.
It's gentleness I've tried to keep
in mind and lost. I find I can remember
no one's affection, though some were kind to me
and some, perhaps, devoted.
                              Passion:
nothing not ferociously imagined, ferociously
executed, has survived.
                              I have become the woman
the lovers I refused had always thought me.

II

Ariana Vanessa Olisvos lies here: born July 22nd,
1881, and died this very day.
          Et In Arcadia Ego
Ariana has gone to the nothingness
her children and her lovers all became
before her; she plotted suicide
so long that it evaded her.

III

No. Say that I died this very night
and had worn out my gallows-humor just before.
Say that I would have held my heart
with both hands
in any furnace of this world to have tomorrow.

Say: Ariana's turned to nothing, maybe . . .
Or, maybe, like many who mightn't've minded hell,
she now suffers in heaven the pangs of forgiveness . . .
And deep in this world she lies, still hungry.

60

Ariana Vanessa McAnn Keller Olisvos
(1881–1975)

On her life:

"Then as to 'biographical information': my verses are wormy with it, and I feel enough like 'a broken bundle of mirrors' that only random glints and splinters of my life catch my eye long enough to seem worth talking of. I was born at sea . . . I am still there. I have been married twice, though only once for pure spite, to men who are both dead now, though only in one of them was the change worth notice or regret. I have kept house and kept an inn and can recommend the latter. I am not what I seem, any more than you are. Like everyone else, I am being tortured to death . . ."

On her book:

"These verses deal with beasts and flowers and with god and other poets and the-worm-in-the-flesh-before-it-dies . . .

"Everything's been written down and I've become (quite deliberately) hard, ungenerous, crueller than I'd thought ever to be. Ninety-some variously delicious years have taught me very little, but at least I no longer expect, even by crossing my path with jests and contradictions, to jam the truth into a sentence.

"These verses are (like every other use to which our dear, obstreperous, embattled language can be put) a tissue of lies and misrepresentations of the obvious truth. They are *not* the poems I began to write, but you are not the woman I began to love and lovingly to make verses of . . .

"And this is not the apology I meant to give you."

Mrs. Olisvos often remarked that she hoped her last words would be, "Who lives by the image shall perish by the word"; they were, in fact, "Good night." She died in her sleep on All Hallows' Eve, 1975; as she had written shortly before, "Like everyone else, she died of natural causes."

61

This book is for Kathleen.

THE
JUNIPER
PRIZE

This volume is the second recipient
of the Juniper Prize,
presented annually by the
University of Massachusetts Press
for a volume of original poetry.
The prize is named in honor of Robert Francis,
who has lived for many years at
Fort Juniper, Amherst, Massachusetts.

Library of Congress Cataloging in Publication Data
Dwyer, David, 1946–
Ariana Olisvos, her last works and days.
"The Juniper prize."
I. Title.
PS3554.W88A9 813'.5'4 76–8752
ISBN 0–87023–217–5
ISBN 0–87023–219–3 pbk.

"These verses deal with beasts and
flowers and with god and other poets
and the worm-in-the-flesh-before-it-dies"
—Ariana Vanessa McAnn Keller Olisvos
(1881-1975)

A poem on her ninety-second birthday,
a letter to her daughter, and reveries of
lost days are some of the markings in
Ariana Olisvos: Her Last Works and Days.
In these lyrical "works," mystery prevails,
ghosts and memories linger, and in the
end, we are left with only Ariana speaking about the book and herself and her
death.

" . . . as to biographical information, my
verses are wormy with it, and I feel
enough like a 'broken bundle of mirrors'
that only random glints and splinters of
my life catch my eye long enough to
seem worth talking of. . . . I am not what
I seem, any more than you are. Like
everyone else, I am being tortured to
death. Everything's been written down
and I've become (quite deliberately) hard,
ungenerous, crueler than I'd thought ever
to be. Ninety-some variously delicious
years have taught me very little, but at
least I no longer expect, even by crossing
my path with jests and contradictions, to
jam the truth into a sentence."

The author, David Dwyer, lives in
Lemmon, South Dakota, where he works
as a farmhand and bartender.

Ariana Olisvos

Her Last Works
and Days